"OBAMA'S
PEOPLE"

"A portion of all book sales will be donated to President Obama's re-election campaign for 2012."

Thank you for your support!

"OBAMA'S PEOPLE"

A New Identity for Biracial

The Biracial and Mixed person's ethnic and national identity... Proud to be an American, self-esteem, happiness, contentment and a model for success.

by: DR. PHILLIP MACFARLAND Ph.D.

To order additional copies of this book, contact:
Xlibris Corporation
1-888-795-4274
www.Xlibris.com
Orders@Xlibris.com
56556

To contact the author about lectures,
Book signings or appearances
please e-mail drpdmac@aol.com or
website www.DrPhillipMacFarland.com

Acknowledgments

I would like to thank God almighty, Jesus, my patron Saints, St Jude, St Michael, The Spirit of Abundance, and The spirits of my ancestors. I would also like to thank the love of my life, Lena, who is my wife, best friend, soul mate, and closest consultant, along with my son Godfrey, my daughters Melason (Raksha), Moria (Roshni), Philecia, and Barbara. A special thanks to my brother Paul who assisted in retrieving the family archival photos, brother Bill, brother Mike, and brother Donald . . . I love you all madly. A special thanks to all of Lena's and my family that allowed me to use their photos. And a special acknowledgement to my grandchildren, colleagues, friends, clients, and the professional staff at Xlibris Publishing. Lastly, I wish to give my wholehearted thanks to President Barack Obama and his family for being the "Eighth Wonder of the World." I have a knowing that he will be the greatest President this country has ever known. Without President Obama being the icon he is, this book could not have been written . . . many thanks and may God bless and keep you and your family

Dr Phillip D. Mac Farland, Ph.D.
Psychologist, Researcher & Author

"An email from President Obama to Dr. Phillip MacFarland" the night he won the election.

How this happened

From: Barack Obama <info@barackobama.com>
To: Phillip MacFarland <drpdmac@aol.com>
Subject: How this happened
Date: Tue, 4 Nov 2008 8:38 pm

Phillip --

I'm about to head to Grant Park to talk to everyone gathered there, but I wanted to write to you first.

We just made history.

And I don't want you to forget how we did it.

You made history every single day during this campaign -- every day you knocked on doors, made a donation, or talked to your family, friends, and neighbors about why you believe it's time for change.

I want to thank all of you who gave your time, talent, and passion to this campaign.

We have a lot of work to do to get our country back on track, and I'll be in touch soon about what comes next.

But I want to be very clear about one thing...

All of this happened because of you.

Thank you,

Barack

Forward

When I was young (before the age of eight) my world and family were almost perfect. I was happy most of the time, felt loved by all, had a very positive outlook on life and enjoyed my day-to-day adventures in the world.

Then after the age of 8, the outside world, mainly the male students at my elementary school, went out of their way to let me know that I was different than them because I was biracial. Somehow in their minds, I was strange and they went out of their way to drive this point home. At this point in my young life, my view of the world changed forever.

As I grew up and later attended college, I earned a terminal degree in clinical psychology (I guess I was trying to figure out myself and other people). Then as today, I feel nothing on this earth is more fascinating than human behavior, so I decided to study it. This is the definition of psychology. It is the study of human behavior. This study has helped me greatly as well as others I have assisted in my role as a psychotherapist and friend.

When I entered my mid-teens, the challenges of being biracial diminished somewhat and I began to make a few and lasting friendships that I cherish to this day. I hope this book will be able to help both the biracial or mixed child, along with the monoracial population of this country that we can all come together as brothers and sisters thanks to our icon, President Barack Obama.

"Obama's People"

The man that made the theme of this book possible

President Barack Obama

Lena . . . my wife . . . the most
beautiful of Obama's people.

Chapter One

Biracial and mixed ethnic groups have a racial/ethnic identity crisis in America.

In president Barack Obama's biographical history, he speaks of going through an identity crisis growing up with an African/Kenyan father and a White/European-American mother, with him being the product of them both but not looking like one or the other. He also grew up in Hawaii for most of his young life and did not look Hawaiian. For a while he also lived in Asia and there too, he did not look Asian and was not able to truly fit in ethnically. Back in the United States, he was not White enough to be considered White, nor Black enough to really be considered Black and as this writer is half African-American (mother of Egyptian, Ethiopian and Creole descent) and Half Scottish-American, we both had an identity crisis early in our formative years. Later, both president Obama and myself have identified ourselves as being African-American, but now we can be more precise about our ethnicity. That is a large part of what this book is about.

When I was a young boy, I was not concerned about my ethnicity at home. I thought it was perfectly normal to grow up with a White father and a Black mother, three White brothers (Bill, Donald and Michael . . . as my father had been previously married to an Irish American woman, but divorced her and gained custody of them) and my brother Paul who, like myself is an offspring of my father and mother. Everything was going along just fine until I reached the age of 8, and my school mates alerted me to the fact that I was different after they saw my mother and father drop me off at school one day. They started asking me,

"What are you?" At first I did not know what they were talking about or referring to. They would ask, "are you Mexican?" I would say no. "Then what are you?" I remember my mother telling me that I was Mulatto, so I told them I was Mulatto (today this label is not politically correct nor a term to be proud of, which I will explain later where this label came from and what it really means). Then again, they would ask . . . "Mulatto? What is that? And by now I had figured out that they had seen my mother and father and where trying to guess where I fit in racially. I then said, matter of factly . . . my father is White and my mother is Negro (this was the early 1950's and Black folks were Negroes in those days). Then they would say . . . . Oh! So you're a half-breed!" As soon as I heard the word I knew it was a bad term and told them not to say that word again. What did I say that for? Now, that was my new name "Half-Breed." And every time I was called that name, I would hit the boy who said it right in the mouth. Needless to say, I think I had one or more fights everyday when I was in elementary school.

In an article written by Charlotte Nitary in a University of Minnesota campus news paper, called "The Leader" . . . "Identity problems in biracial youth" . . . she states the following: While there is little data on the number of biracial children in the US, there is a consensus among demographers that we are experiencing a "biracial baby boom." According to the 1990 U.S. Census, there were approximately 800,000 interracial families with about one million biracial children in the country (Herring, 1995) [that was some 13-years ago at this writing]. Biracial youth have a very unique problem that most of their peers never experience: a racial identity crisis. These biracial youth have difficulties identifying what they are in society.

Historically, children of mixed parentage were identified with the parent of color; if one parent was black, then the child was considered black. While such simplification may have been adequate in the past, studies are showing that more and more biracial children in today's society are experiencing identity problems [hopefully with President Obama's presidency and this book, this identity problem will be resolved].

The Grand Cotillion had its American Origin in New Orleans in the French Quarter, son Godfrey, niece Krystal, Obama's Finest.

What is racial identity?

Bradshaw (1992) claims that developing a healthy self-esteem and an integrated sense of self is more complex for the biracial person than the monoracial person. Since health identity development is crucial to the formation of a normal personality, the issue of identity of children of mixed heritage is critical (Milan & Kelley, 2000). According to Fore-Marzul (1994), identity grows on three levels of all human development:

- Physical
- Psychological
- Cultural:

The nurturing of self-identity is a prime function of the family. An example of that is that in our society, the developmental needs of Black children are significantly different from those of White children.

Black children are taught, from an early age, highly sophisticated coping techniques to deal with racist practices perpetrated by individuals and institutions. Some studies show that only a Black family can transmit the emotional and sensitive subtleties of perception and reaction essential for a black child's survival in a racist society.

Racial identity problems arise when biracial children have to face choosing one racial group and rejecting the other in order to develop an identity. We live in a society that sees things as Black or White, with no gray areas. Tiger Woods, who is part African American and part Asian, says that society does not give these children a chance to embrace every aspect of their heritage. Forde-Marul (1994) also points out that, although American society has historically defined biracial people (from Black and White parents) as Black, it is questionable whether Black people, as a rule, view biracial people in this way. He says that, in fact, biracial children can experience rejection and alienation from Black people as well as from White people.

Wardle (1989) says that today, parents assume one of three positions as to the identity of their interracial children. Some insist that their child is "human above all else" and that race or ethnicity is irrelevant, while others choose to raise their children with the identity of the parent of color. Another growing group of parents is insisting that the child have the ethnic, racial, cultural and genetic heritage of both parents.

According to Wardle (1989), experts do not agree as to what the biracial child identity should be. Some believe an interracial child should have the identity of the parent of color because historically that has been the case, and also because society "sees" these children as having the identity of the parent of color. However, others have argued that the identity of any child is based on an accurate presentation of his or her true background—a child should know, for example, that his "white" mother has a Scottish heritage while his "black" father claims African, Native American and Asian roots.

The Legal definition of RACE

Government forms do not have a "biracial" category. Biracial organizations are seeking to have a status of biracial children formally recognized and included in the U.S. Census. Courtney (1995) says that job applications, survey forms, college-entrance exams, all ask individuals to check only one box for race. She says "For most of my life, I have marked black because my skin color is the first thing people notice. One of the greatest things parents of biracial children can do is expose them to both of their cultures. But what good does this do when in the end society makes us choose? Having a separate category marked "biracial" will not magically put an end to the pressure to choose, but it will help people to stop judging us as just black or just white and see us for what we really are—both."

"A Real Bi-racial Family and it's Roots"

Dad's side of the Family in the late 1800's in Oregon and Mom's side of the family in Los Angeles in the 1950's.

Obama's People

The MacFarland Clan, grandmother, Mac, Dad MacFarland, then L to R: Donald, Paul, Mike, Phil and Bill. All brothers. Obama's People.

Ramona Douglass, president of the Association of Multiethnic Americans (whose parents are Italian and African-American/Native American, says her organization is lobbying for a "multiracial" designation on government forms not because we and others are trying to "step out of our African-American heritage," but because historically, the U.S. has been racist in the classifications. "I am not simply an African-American," she says. "I am a mixture of all my heritages. I see no reason to deny any part of myself."

Their battle is far from being won. Not surprisingly, the notion of drastically altering the nation's racial demographics is meeting opposition from civil rights organizations and major segments of the African-American community. There is concern that political strength will be diluted of the tens of thousands of biracial individuals now considered Black are recategorized as a separate ethnic group (Norment, 1995). Townsel (1996) also supports this by saying that the leaders in the black community are outraged because it would threaten affirmative action and EEO programs since the data collected through the census are used to monitor these programs. Dr. Halford Fairchild, associate professor of psychology and Black studies at Pitzer College in Claremont, Calif., is biracial as well as agrees that the government's classifications have a legacy steeped in racism. But he emphasizes that a multiracial designation on census forms could have the negative effect of reducing the size of the Black population, "which could have dire political consequences."

The National Association of Black Social Workers has influenced the American court system by arguing that biracial children should be treated as completely black. Consistent with this view, courts and adoption agencies usually categorize biracial children as black when considering placement. The primary justification for this treatment is that, in the eyes of American society, a biracial child is black and, therefore, must identify positively with being black and must be able to cope with discrimination toward her[him] as a black person. The NABSW also opposes placing biracial children with white parents. The NABSW argues that society and those around such children will treat them as Black and, consequently, these children also need to identify positively as Black and cope with racial prejudice. As a result, the NABSW (National Association of Black Social Workers) concludes that when an adoption of custody proceeding concerns a biracial child, a court or adoption agency should favor placing the child with Black parents (Forde-Mazrui, 1994)

She also warns the court that, by treating a biracial child as black, the court decide first, the biracial child should identify herself[himself] as only one race, and second, that this race should be black. For a biracial child, who needs exposure to both racial backgrounds, and who needs to accept both cultural heritages, choosing an all-black identity may contribute to a certain degree of identity confusion and self-rejection.

Recommendations to Educators

Biracial youth need the regular positive youth development offered to other youth such as support empowerment, mentoring [such as the great image of President Barack Obama which is monumental] etc, however, they need additional attention. Educators should have programs that meet the needs of affirming identity for these youths (McDonough, 1998) [it is also hoped that President Obama will be sensitive to this issue and encourage federal forms to now include two categories of 1.)Biracial-American and 2.) mixed heritage-American].

In order to work effectively with children and their families, people in the helping professions must be sensitive to a wide variety of issues and factors that contribute to a child's behavior and well being. Children of mixed racial or ethnic parentage also have unique needs—but often the professionals who work with these children in day care centers, schools, or social services or health care settings . . . lack the training or awareness to provide the best possible services, support, and encouragement to these children and their families (Wardle, 1989).

Wardle (1989) provides specific things that family educators can do to work effectively with interracial children and families:

- Support the parent's right to be part of a mixed marriage. Provide support, counseling and referral based on the individual needs of the family or child.

- Educators should not automatically assume that an interracial child has the identity only of the parent of color. Many interracial parents are still searching for a true identity for their children, and a caring professional can give them an opportunity to examine their options by providing them with resources.

- Provide parents and children with tools, such as the right words, to defend and protect themselves from others who don't appreciate differences and help families feel proud of their mixed heritage [today with President Barack Obama being the president of the United States and the most powerful man in the world at this time, will definitely help biracials & mixed heritage children & adults to feel proud of their heritage.]

- Do not automatically attribute a child's problems to his or her mixed heritage. Children have many developmental tasks to accomplish, including developing a healthy self-concept, and any of these can cause problems for the child. Explore causes that are not related to identity first [and also include a statement about society's need for education on this issue and they have been grossly ignorant on this issue].

- Support interracial families, and encourage programs serving such families, to provide a variety of books, music, dolls, art materials and other materials that reflect a rich variety of the family backgrounds. For instance, preschool classrooms should have black, white and biracial dolls, and posters that don't divide the world into only white, black, Hispanic [Asian] and Native American people.

References:

Bradshaw, C. 1992. "Beauty and the Beast": On Racial Ambiguity in Racially Mixed People in American, Newbury Park, CA: Sage.

Forde-Mazrui, K. (1994). Black identity and child placement: the best interests of black and biracial children. Michigan Law Review, 92(4), 925-967.

Courtney, B., (1995). Freedom from choice; being biracial has meant denying half my identity. Newsweek, 125(7), 16.

Gordon, Milton M. 1978. Human Nature, Class, and Ethnicity. New York: Oxford University Press.

Herring, R. (1995). Developing biracial ethnic identity: A review of the increasing dilemma. Journal of Multicultural Counseling and Development, 23, 29-38.

Jaret, C. & Reitzes, D. (1999). The importance of racial-ethnic identity and social setting for blacks, whites, and multiracials. Sociological Perspectives, 42(4), 711.

Luke, C., Carrington, V., (2000). Race Matters. Journal of Intercultural Studies, 21, 5.

McDonough, K. (1998). Can the Liberal State Support Cultural Identity Schools? American Journal of Education, 463(1).

Milan, S., & Keiley, M. (2000). Biracial youth and families in therapy: Issues and interventions. Journal of Marital and Family Therapy. 26 (3) 305.

Norment, L. (1995). Am I black, white or in between? Is there a plot to create a 'colored' buffer race in America? Ebony 50 (10), 108.

Saenz, R., Hwang, S., Aguirre, B. & Anderson, N. (1995). Persistence and change in Asian identity among children of intermarried couples. Sociological Perspectives, 38 (2) 175.

Townsel, L. (1996). 'Neither black nor white.' (mixed race people demand new census race category). Ebony, 52(1), 44.

Wardle, F. (1989). Children of mixed parentage; how can professionals respond? Children Today, 18 (4) 10.

Charlotte Nitardy is a candidate in the administrative licensure program for school superintendents and a doctoral student in the Department of Work, Community, and Family Education. She holds a M.Ed. in human resource development and my acknowledgement and thanks goes out to her for the contribution she has made to this book.

Chapter Two

Little did President Obama know that he would become the answer to his own identity crisis and for all the biracial people in this country and the world. By President Barack Obama being the most powerful man in the world, at this writing, he has created an identity for BiRacials and all people of mixed heritage to be very proud of and one leader we can identify with in a very positive way. BiRacials and mixed people now have a clear identity . . . we are now called *"Obama's People."*

So today if anyone asks a biracial or mixed person what they are, they can proudly say, I am an American and "I am **one of Obama's people**." That's who and what I am.

Since President Obama's biography has been both seen and read around the world, when the term *Obama's People* is stated, people are now clear on the individual's ethnic identity.

During President Obama's run for the presidency, both America and the entire world watched with close attention to see how he presented himself, his background and family history, education, his persona as a person of color and being an American. Americans were impressed with his calm but attentive demeanor, his keen intellect, and his presidential presence even as a candidate. He just conducted himself like a president versus his several opponents, as well as Senator McCain.

President Obama had initially authored a number of books prior to his candidacy which spoke of hope (the

Audacity of Hope) and his rise to the White House. Not only America was watching, but the whole world was watching and hoping for a real change.

The world saw that Barack Obama was an eloquent speaker, very intelligent, a Harvard graduate, cool under fire, and an inspiring husband and father image. He also was smart enough to make use of 21st century technology (via the computer) and an unstoppable grass-roots ground campaign, which included organizing all segments and age groups of our society. He and his team organized the Obama movement in a way that no other political figure has ever done. He had a new impact on younger people and those that had never voted or were going to be voting for the first time. His campaign looked like a rainbow of people, ethnic groups, genders, sexual orientations, and all age groups, with a lot of support from young educated adults.

In assessing this great movement and dynamic, Obama had a way of bringing all groups together and this is the essence of this book. When you really look at who is biracial nowadays, and especially the subject of who is mixed in America. Almost everybody is mixed in America. If you set aside the Black and White racial mixture issue and you just look at ethnic groups, and nationality mixing . . . even among whites, America is unique. Many whites in America are half Irish and half French, half German & half Italian or even more mixtures if you toss Native American ancestry. However, in Europe, it is more common that French marry French, English marry English, Germans marry Germans, Italians marry Italians and so on. This same ethic group paring is not nearly as common in America where all ethnicities and races have come together in just a few hundred years since America has been a sovereign nation. President Obama has now brought most of America together both as Americans and ethnically . . . we are more united than ever before in our history. Because of President Obama's personal history, example, and now **referent power,** he has made this new identity possible.

Proud of our nephew: Justin Kelley, handsome,
graduate of Arizona State University and one
of "Obama's People."

Niece Jamila Kelley, another one of Obama's People. Beautiful, intelligent, and a college graduate of UC Davis.

A special moment with Grammy Lena and granddaughter Maya at The Palace Garden Court in SF.

Chapter Three

Referent Power and the
5 Bases of Social Power

President Obama is now the president of the United States and also the most powerful man in the world. This is the ultimate power that a man can have on planet earth. I will attempt to give a detailed description of this power in this chapter.

In the field of psychology and sociology the term referent power describes a person of high status and admiration with which one or more people associate themselves. It is individual power based on a high level of identification with, admiration of, or respect for the power holder: Nationalism, Patriotism,

Celebrity, and well-respected people are examples of Referent Power in effect. It is the power or ability of an individual to attract others and build loyalty. It's based on charisma and interpersonal skills of the power holder. Here the people under this power desire to identify with these personal qualities, and gains satisfaction from being an accepted follower. Nationalism, Patriotism and Ethnicity counts towards an intangible sort of referent power as well. For example, soldiers fight in wars to defend the honor of their country.

Referent power is one of the five components of *social power. In reviewing all 5 bases of social power, it is clear that President Obama has them all.* They are as follows: **Positional Power;** also called "Legitimate Power" . . . it refers to power of an individual because of the relative position and duties of the holder of the position with an organization. Legitimate power is formal authority delegated to the holder of the position. It is usually accompanied by various attributes of power such as a high office, title, etc. This is the most obvious and also the most important kind of power. Being the commander in chief of the most powerful military in the world, for example.

Expert Power: expert power is an individual's power deriving from the skills or expertise of the person and the organization's need (The Federal Government as President) for those skills and expertise (a constitutional Law attorney, a Harvard Law School Graduate, a State and US Senator and now as America's number one leader).

Information Power: While difference between expert power and information power is subtle, people with this type of power are well informed, up-to-date and also have the ability to persuade others. They also have the latest information, military secrets, knowledge of superior weaponry, and have confidence in debating and are persuasive.

Reward Power: Reward power depends upon the ability of the power wielder to confer valued material or status rewards; it refers to the degree to which the individual can give others a reward of some kind such as: The Congressional Medal of Honor, a presidential pardon, an endorsement for a political position, an appointment to a high position in the presidential cabinet for example.

Coercive Power: Coercive power means the application of negative influences onto others or to unleash the power of one's military might upon a foe. Or fear of having benefits or money withheld. This type of power must be used very judiciously.

These are all the powers President Barack Obama has at his disposal, but for the purpose of this book, being identified ethnically with such a powerful and intelligent man now gives a clear identity to people of Biracial and mixed heritage . . . . "Obama's People."

For example, when Winston Churchill inspired and led the British to overcome the challenges of World War II and Nazi Germany's determination to destroy England and failed. The English readily identified with Churchill and were very proud to be British under his leadership. They were honored to be considered "Churchill's people."

When Nelson Mandela an Ethnic Black South African Attorney who sought to fight for the rights of Black South Africans from the cruel discrimination of the Apartheid White run government, he was unjustly imprisoned for over 20-years of his life. Then by the will of the people and fair-minded nations around the world (through boycotts), put pressure on the oppressive government to release Mandela who later became the first Black leader and president of South Africa since the days of colonization. Both Black and White Africans and Afrikaans applauded his leadership and determination. Both Black, Coloureds and Whites became Mandela's people and were proud to be called South Africans under his leadership and legacy.

When people feel like they belong to such leaders, mentors and progressive idealists are due to their social power, intellect, charisma and love of the people.

Now President Obama has referent and social power even though he comes from humble beginnings. Having been born to a young White mother from Kansas and having an African father from Kenya . . . he was born into a society that did not embrace this kind of union, nor the off-spring of their interracial union.

I remember my mother telling me when I was a teenager, that she and my father had to get married 3-times before their marriage was legal as my mother was of African descent and my father was of Scottish descent. During the 1940's, a marriage between a White man and Black woman was not legally recognized by California law. My mother told me that after she and my father had gotten married in California, and about 6-months later they received a letter in the mail stating that their marriage was not recognized as legal. Hence, they were not legally married. My parents then went to Reno, Nevada and were married for a second time. A few months later they again received a second letter that marriages between Blacks and Whites were not recognized or legal in the state of Nevada. Being at their wits end and my mother being unwilling to be in a relationship as a "shack up job" (as it was called in those days), my parents hired a family law attorney to find out where a Black woman and White man that loved each other, could be legally get married in the United States of the America.

Mom and Dad MacFarland . . .
Obama's People

As my parents lived in the San Francisco Bay area at the time, the attorney told them that the nearest place for them to go to be legally married was Albuquerque, New Mexico. So they got on a plane and flew to New Mexico to be married for the third time for their marriage to be legally recognized. My mother went on to say that she and my father wore out their marriage license showing it to people (such as hotel and restaurant operators) to prove that they were married, that they could patronize their establishments. There were some establishments, even in the State of California, where Blacks were not allowed; however, if she was married to a White man and legally married (by producing a valid marriage license) most times, they would allow both of my parents to patronize the hotel or restaurant. My parents have laid claim to being the first legally married Black and White couple in the State of California in the early 1940's (William and Evelyn Nabila MacFarland). They were the pioneers of change just as President Obama is the pioneer of change in America and the world today.

Now that Biracials and mixed individuals have a clear and proud identity through President Obama, we must move to a higher level of action, set aside the notion that "no we can't" and embrace Obama's mantra "yes we can." And now with a clear identity and pride, President Obama has proven that we can do anything, we must roll up our sleeves and make the impossible . . . possible. If you want proof, look at today's president of the United States. **Yes we can!**

"Obama's People"

Godfrey and Nicole with their baby

"Aribella"

(which means *beautiful prayer and she is*)

Photo by Ryan Young

"Obama's People"
Bridging the Racial Divide
Photo by Ryan Young

Son Godfrey, escorts Le Gran Dame,

Grandma Rose.

Diversity within the family: Here are brother and sister Kenneth Arline and Deborah Arline-Kelley

Mo'mi, Auntie and Aribella (a beautiful prayer) "Obama's People."

Dad MacFarland with T-Bone Walker at our home, one of the greatest Blues Guitarists in the World, also playing the piano.

The Famous Duo "Salt and Pepper" singing
our way through college, Humboldt County:
Redwood Country,

He's Pepper   I'm Salty

Ramada Inn McKinleyville, 1974
Humboldt State University

In President Obama's 2004 Democratic Convention speech, he stated the following: "I stand here today, grateful for the diversity of my heritage, aware that my parents' dreams live on in my precious daughters. I stand here knowing that my story is part of a larger American story, that I owe a debt to all of those who came before me, and that, in no other country on earth, is my story even possible." And now Barack Obama is the President of the United States of America and also the most powerful man in the world. Biracials and mixed persons in the United States and all over the world now have someone that they can identify with ethnically, and continue to be proud of who we really are.

I do not want to get into my own autobiography, for that is material for another book, but like President Obama, I can only say that, only in America can a story like mine also be possible. From my own humble beginnings growing up in one of the toughest neighborhoods in the country, (North Richmond, California) having a loving college-educated stay-at-home mother and a hard working blue-collar father, and with my wife, Lena's encouragement, that I am able to write this book as Dr Phillip MacFarland, Licensed Clinical Psychologist, with a PhD, three masters degrees and a BA.

I can speak with some fluency in seven different languages, have traveled half of the world, married to a former model and actress, live in an affluent gated community, drive luxurious cars, and most importantly, live during a time when Barack Obama is the president of the United States of America and is, at this writing, the most powerful man in the world. Now is the time for *all U.S. citizens* to be proud and most grateful to be an American. We are now truly living the pronouncement of our founding fathers that "All Men [and women] are created equal" in America.

President Obama has not only brought biracial and mixed people in the United States together, but also others of mixed birthright around the world. One clear model of this is when American soldiers attempt to bring Democracy to others around the world such as Japan, Korea, Viet Nam, Kuwait, Iraq, Panama, Cuba, the Philipines and more. You will find the children of these soldiers and also Americans who travel extensively, falling in love with women and American women falling in love with men from these countries, most times marrying them and having mixed children. Many of these children have been ostracized if the father has not brought them back to America, or they are looked down upon in their own country. But now with President Obama symbolizing the greatness that can come from a biracial union, he now has begun to bring an identity to these beautiful biracial and mixed children around the world. It is for this reason and more that President Obama is a uniter and not a divider for America and the world.

Lena And Doc at the Palace Hotel Garden

Court, San Francisco, California

Chapter Four

President Obama is a uniter not a divider and I want to make one point perfectly clear. With the president now giving a positive identity to biracials and people of mixed heritage does not in any way detract from his connection to black and white people or mine. Nor does it make any ethnic group less than biracials or mixed groups. The phenomena of a clear ethnic identity created by President Obama, in my opinion, is that it helps today's BiRacials or mixed persons to not have to go into a five-minute oratory of what ethnicity or nationality they are. Or what race or ethnicity their parents are. This is what biracials and mixed people have had to put up with in the past. Today all we need to

say, to have folks understand our ethnic identity is . . . .
"I am one of Obama's people" and more importantly . . .
I am an American. That's it!

BiRacials and mixed groups now have a quick and positive identity as many other mixed ethnic groups have enjoyed . . . such as: Mexicans (primarily Amerindians and Spanish, Filipinos (Negritos the indigenous people, Chinese, Spanish, Malaysian), Puerto Ricans (Spanish, African, & Caribbean Indians) and today's Hawaiians (Hawaiian, Chinese, Japanese, other island groups and European groups). So the advantage that these particular nationalities or ethnic groups have had is a readily identifiable group with which they belong via language, custom and culture, without having to go into detail as to their diverse ethnic mixture.

The MacFarland Clan (L to R) Maya, Godfrey, Lena, Doc, Melason (Raksha) and Moria (Roshni) . . . "Obama's People" at the Ritz Carlton Presidential Suite Half-Moon Bay, CA.

Three sisters and three colors, very
light (Deborah), tan (Lena), and brown
(Minette) . . . Obama's People.

"Big Auntie" The matriarch of the family. Now 92 and still working in her own business . . . "Obama's People" Mrs. McMahan Lena's Aunt

Parents of biracial children may have a confounding challenge in terms of how they will teach their children to identify themselves in terms of their societal persona (how the outside American society perceives them ethnically). In the home, children are clear that they are half Black and Half white or half this and half that, whatever the mixture is. But when the child goes out into society, many times they are asked, what I was asked as a young child, . . . "what are you?" Now parents can educate their children to clearly be proud of both racial sides of their family as I was. I was taught that I received the best from both sides of the family. My father's people were pioneers that help settle this country and were part of the land grant settlers of the Oregon territory. My mother's people were educators and revolutionized agriculture in the South (the introduction of Egyptian cotton) and the richness of the Creole culture. So biracial and mixed children do not have to go into a 5-minute oratory to explain "what they are. They can proudly say and to society . . . " I am one of Obama's people" and a proud American. That's all that needs to be said.

In traveling to Europe, biracials and other mixed groups don't seem to have the identity issue as much as they have in the United States. I have found that growing up in the United States and being Biracial, people want to know your ethnic make up or racial composition. However, in Europe . . . the Europeans can tell what you are after a few minutes of watching you and listening to you. They will tell you . . . "Oh, you are American." Foreigners appear to be able to identify us more clearly than we do our own as Americans.

I remember one time when I was in Zurich Switzerland; I was to meet a businessman whom I had only spoken to over the telephone. We had partnered in a business deal and I was to meet him at the Zurich airport in front of a Tobacco & Magazine shop. Not knowing what I looked like, he walked right up to me and asked if I was Phillip MacFarland and I said yes, are you Harry T . . . ?, and he said yes. I then asked how did he recognize me? He stated that "I knew you were American because you are rather tall and big "blokes," the way you dress, carry yourselve, the way you talk, and you guys are always chewing gum." He paid no attention that I had tanned skin, dark wavy/curly hair. It was a strange experience to have a strange foreigner tell me who I really was . . . an American. As I traveled around Europe people could tell I was American by my size (six-foot two-inches tall and 250 lbs) and by the type of English I spoke . . . American English. Not British English, not New Zealand English, not Australian English or Canadian English. The other things, which set us Americans apart from other people in Europe, is that we Americans ask for "ice" for our drinks. As soon as you ask for ice for your drink, many servers in restaurants will say, "Oh yes . . . you are American . . . I should have known. Also if you ask for a straw or a sack to put your baguette of bread. For many Europeans, especially the French will buy a baguette of bread place it under there arm and walk away without a sack. These are things we are not mindful of when traveling throughout the United States. In Europe, it really made me feel good inside and proud when the British, French, Spanish, Italians and Dutch would call me . . . American. It was an interesting finding for me to understand that most Europeans see people of color from the United States as Americans, while our fellow American citizens focus on whatever ethnic group or race we may belong to from their perception. It was a good experience for me to be called an American. I came to know from my travels that this is also my primary identity . . . being an American and I am very proud to be one and I am oh so glad, to have been born in America.

Chapter Five

"A pictorial"

Another unique phenomenon of biracial couples, biracials, or mixed people is that we may all have the same mother and father but the children may come out with a variety of colors and features. We have seen in president Obama's family, he looks different than his sister even though were born from the same mother. Clearly this difference in complexions and features is also present in my and my wife's family. Many same race couples and families can't understand this dynamic, so to help them gain a better understanding,

I have included a pictorial of both my wife's and my family via photos we have in both of our family trees.

See the Beautiful Rainbow of people in our biracial and mixed families in the following photos.

Sister and brother-in-law Deborah and Wayne Kelley

Obama's People

"Margie" . . . Great grandmother of Lena MacFarland late 1800's, dreaming of the day that a man like Obama would be president . . . Yes We Can!

Mom MacFarland, with Phillip in her arm, brother Michael, and below brother Paul, Richmond, CA, 1949. Below: Grandmother MacFarland and her 5 grandsons 1952.
. . . . **Obama's People**

Cultural Diversity in the Family: Dad MacFarland's people in 1898: Uncle Charley, Uncle Joe, Aunt Dorothy and Aunt Margaret and (below) Mom MacFarland and Her Family in the 1950's

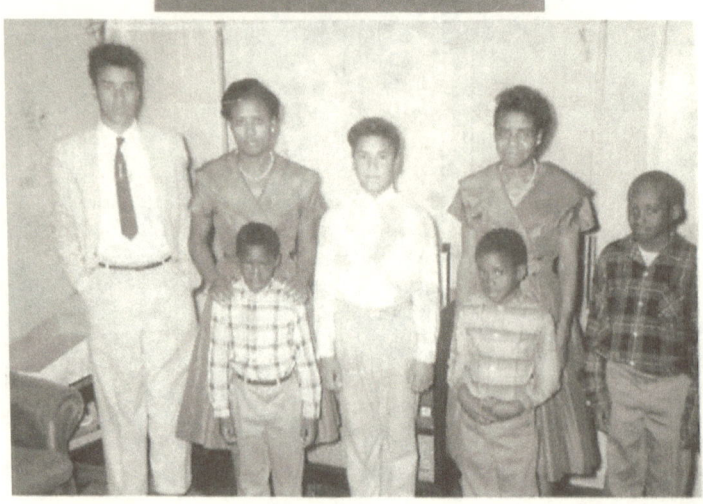

Our Three grandchildren, Maya & Makoto Motomura
(brother and sister) and Mateo/Mathew Lopez (their
cousin)

Mateo's Party

Nephew Derek MacFarland and wife Sarah, Ogden, Utah

Obama's People

The Three Brothers and nephews at Brother Bill's Idaho ranch
Left to right: Phil, Andrew, Bro Bill, (holding the MacFarland family crest) Darin, and Bro Paul

L to R: Bro Bill, Darcy, Darron, Phil, Lena, Sonny Andrew Bro Paul, Carol & Bro Mike

Eldest of the MacFarland Clan, brother
Bill and wife MaeFrancis
Obama's People

Chapter Six

This chapter will review some research and origins of biracial people by country, and history over time. What does history tell us about biracial people and where they came from? In looking back at history, and the topic of the origin of biracial people, no data is available which gives us a clear understanding of where it all began. However, a good starting point is reviewing the travels of conquering nations as Rome, Egypt, the Greeks, Arabs, The Portuguese, Spanish, Dutch and the British.

Starting with the Roman Empire, the Romans had one of the most powerful armies in history during their reign of power. It was also common for Roman aristocrats to have slaves of all colors, including African, East Indian and Middle Eastern people of color, as well as northern European slaves. The intermingling of these groups with the Romans was possibly the first biracial groups in a major society in written history. Additionally, there was the Roman military that granted Roman soldiers the right to enjoy the "spoils of war" after they may had conquered a village, town or country. Some of these spoils included the woman of these conquered areas, many of whom were woman of color that had babies by these Roman soldiers. The children of these women would have been considered biracial.

If we review Roman history research the countries they conquered and occupied, a number of them were in sub-Saharan Africa, the Middle East, East India, and Turkey. Of course the offspring from these women would be considered biracial.

Another very powerful group which conquered nations were the Arab groups that have commonly been referred to as the Moors. The Moors had far and wide conquests throughout the Middle East, parts of Asia and as far north as Ireland and the British Isles. When an Arab male had a child by a darker skinned woman (non-Arab) the child would be given the name *Muwallad*, which means "a person of mixed ancestry." The word also means "born, begotten, produced, generated; brought up, raised; born and raised among Arabs (but not of pure Arab blood).

The Portuguese also engaged in the slave trade of Africans, Asians and the indigenous people of South America, especially Brazil. They identified a word for Biracials called *mestico* which was commonly used in Brazil and Cape Verde where the Portuguese had racially mixed with the Africans and also the indigenous people (Amerindians) whom they controlled through colonization and slavery.

The term *mulatto* is not commonly used anymore in today's Brazilian society. Instead they use the term *Moreno* . . . light Moreno, dark Moreno to denote people that are of mixed blood in Brazil. However,

May 13th is Mulatto Day in Brazil and is celebrated as a holiday. It denotes the struggle to abolish slavery in Brazil with the signing of the freedom proclamation call the Lei Aurea, on May 13th, 1888, which abolished slavery in Brazil [some 23-years after slavery was abolished in the United States]. The term *mulatto* taken from the Wikipedia encyclopedia is used to describe a person with one White parent and one Black parent or a person whose ancestry is a mixture of Black and White. The term *mulatto* is perceived as a pejorative and demeaning term in some cultures. Its current usage varies and is little used in the U.S. anymore.

Etymology

The etymology of the word mulatto is uncertain. It could have been derived from the Portuguese or Spanish as the term can also mean "a small mule," which in itself is derived from "mulo" Mule; from

Old Spanish; from Latin Mul'us, by analogy with the mule, which is a hybrid an offspring of a horse and a donkey. It was once a generic designation name for any hybrid.

Therefore biracials consider the term *mulatto* offensive and most biracials in the U.S. usually identify themselves as being Black or biracial.

Latin America and the Caribbean

Mulattoes or biracials represent a significant portion of the various countries' populations in Latin America: (The Dominican Republic 73%), Cuba (51%), Venezuela (30%), Brazil (38.5%), Puerto Rico (11%), Belize (25%), Colombia (14%) and Haiti (up to 5%)

Mexico

There were 200,000 Africans brought to Mexico but most have been absorbed by the mestizo populations of mixed European ancestry (primarily Spanish) and some Amerindian descent. The State of Guerro once had a large population of African slaves. Other Mexican states were inhabited by people with some African ancestry, along with other ancestries which include Oaxoca, Veracruz and Yucata'n.

So as one can see by reading the introduction of Africans to areas throughout the world, we have seen the development of numerous biracial/mixed groups in a large portion of the world, especially in the Western Hemisphere.

[Reference: Guest Editorial, The Interracial Voice Journal: Mullato, A Definition & The Evolution of Identity by Liam Martin and Journal Editor and Chief, Charles Byrd.]

Chapter Seven

An Ethnic Commonality between the Ancient Romans and today's Americans

The ancient Roman Empire was huge geographically and had its armies and commerce spread throughout the known world at that time. Africa, Asia Minor, Europe (Germany, France, and Spain), as well as the British Isles . . . and more. Rome was filled with people from these areas of the world and was a multi-ethnic metropolis.

Today, America is also composed of people from Europe, Africa, Asia and the British Isles, as well as

Native Americans, Mexicans, people from the Pacific Isles, and the Caribbean.

As a consequence of the Romans being in so many places around the world, it is human that a mixing of the races took place. Many of these people came to Rome for reasons of commerce, the arts, entertainment, education, as slaves, or to claim the City of Rome as their home. If you could have observed the complexions and features of the people that inhabited Rome in those ancient days, they have appeared very diverse, as they were made up of many races, ethnic groups, and cultures. Much like America's people today.

Therefore, the ancient Romans were not a clear defined race of people, but rather they may have looked similar to the ancient Greeks (that had African, Asian, Arab, Egyptian and European mixtures). This would have given the masses of Roman people the appearance of North-African, Sephardic Jews, people of the Middle-East, as well as groups from Asia and India.

A person can easily find this same diverse group of people in the United States, especially in our major metropolitan cities (New York, Atlanta, Miami, Chicago, Seattle, San Francisco, Los Angeles and New Orleans, just to name a few.

The Roman Empire was very expansive and had trade routes in Asia, Africa, India, Greece and Europe. Similarly, America has had lots of contact with these same countries through war, immigration, slavery, and general commerce. America has had additional racial and ethnic contact with the indigenous people of the America's . . . Amer-Indians, Pacific Islanders, and the people of the Caribbean. All these people now inhabit America and the mixing of these groups have taken place. So, we Americans are even more diverse than the Ancient Romans may have been, with the addition of these additional groups that Rome had not made contact.

On a more personal note, my wife, Lena and I were in Rome in 2004, and we had our pictures taken in front of the Ancient Roman Coliseum, along with a Roman that was dressed as a Roman Centurion. He stood along side of us in taking the picture (see the picture we took at the Coliseum in his book). As I reviewed the picture, I could not help but notice that our complexions were quite similar and his general features were similar to my wife and I, whom are of mixed heritage. So even the appearance of Roman citizens today, are similar to us Americans of mixed heritage and race. Here is another commonality between the ancient Romans and Americans of diverse backgrounds.

My wife and I are of diverse ethnic and racial backgrounds and we seem to fit right in during our tour of Rome and its citizens. Additionally, when I began speaking some Italian to the locals, we were treated more as Italians than American tourists. They took us into their homes, made provincial meals for us and took us to special sites that most tourists rarely go. After this experience, I remembered as passage in the New Testament Bible, "When in Rome, do as the Romans."

Lena and Doc at the Coliseum in Rome. We now have the sword.

"When in Rome, do as the Romans."

The Queen Mary II maiden voyage to the Mediterranean and our 25th Wedding Anniversary/Renewing our vows in Athens Greece 2004.

So, being a Roman in ancient times was not a matter of a racial identity, but rather it was cultural in nature. It must have been a similar cultural mix which exists in America today. Just think about it. There is no race called American, but there is definitely a unique American Culture that differentiates Americans from other Nationalities through our, language (American English), music, foods, holidays, our dress, sports, and government. This diversity in America is primarily based on the diverse populations that came to America and brought their languages, food, education, cultural activities and more. This is what created a blended America or what has been commonly referred to as a "melting pot." This is why we have celebrations of Cinco de Mayo, Columbus Day, Kwanza, Hanukah, October Fest, Smorgasbord, Mardi Gras and more. This diversity is what it means to be an American. This diversity is also once again, what makes us "Obama's People."

We are diverse, but we are all one. For we are not made up of a White America, or A Black America, nor a Brown or Red America, but rather "The United People of America . . . "Obama's People."

A good term to insert right here is a word called . . . "Synergy." The word comes from the Greek language which is called *synergia*. This means joint work or cooperative action. Synergy occurs when the result of a group is greater than the sum of its individual parts. Synergy is created when things work in concert together to create an outcome that is in some way, more valuable or efficient than singular individual inputs. What we don't need is a bunch of individuals running around trying to accomplish goals singularly. This is what President Obama created in his election campaign and it is my belief that this is what he will continue to create and inspire during his presidency . . . Synergism. The tremendous benefit of Americans working together and setting aside out petty individual issues to work for the common good of the country.

We Americans have finally come together with our diversity and unique contributions, in a synergistic way, to create a national 'Human Bouquet" for success in all domains of American life. In the areas of leadership, research, education, technology, energy, medicine, religion, commerce, culture and diplomacy. By further uniting as Americans and as "Obama's People", we can accomplish anything. Lets do it!

A Final Word:

"Our deepest fear is not that we are inadequate. Our deepest fear is that we are powerful beyond measure. It is our light, not our darkness that most frightens us. We ask ourselves . . . Who am I to be brilliant, gorgeous, talented, fabulous? Actually, who are you not to be? You are a child of God. You playing small does not serve the world. There is nothing enlightened about shrinking so that other people won't feel insecure around you . . . as we let our own light shine, we unconsciously give other people permission to do the same. As we are liberated from our own fear, our presence automatically liberates others."

by Marianne Williamson

Thank you

www.ingramcontent.com/pod-product-compliance
Lightning Source LLC
Chambersburg PA
CBHW031246280526
45784CB00004B/1741